APOCALYPSE

Meditations on the Revelation of John
in Word and Picture

ANNEKE KAAI

DEDICATED TO

MY PARENTS,

HUSBAND AND CHILDREN

LITERARY

PRESENTATION

PIET KROLIS

One generation will commend your works to another;
they will tell of your mighty acts.
They will speak of the glorious splendour of your majesty,
and I will meditate on your wonderful works.
They will tell of the power of your awesome works,
and I will proclaim your great deeds.

Ps. 145:4-6

INTRODUCTION

The culmination of God's plan for this world is described in the last book of the Bible, the Book of Revelation. It comprises twenty-two chapters, two of which contain the letters to the seven Churches. The remaining twenty chapters record a series of visions, and it was these visions which provided the source of my inspiration.

Difficulties are often encountered in trying to understand the visions as they are formidable, both in number and nature. It was this very problem, that gave me the impetus to portray them. With God's help, this series of twenty-four paintings has resulted. They have been painted with oils on silk, and mixed media have been used to try and convey the radiance of the visions.

The actual work of painting was preceded by considerable study which was necessary to give expression to the visions. I have tried to depict the visions as completely as possible so that almost all the details of the Biblical text are shown. In this way these paintings provide an image of the Book of Revelation. The purpose of this work is therefore to bring the Bible closer to the reader.

The personal reason for my work is to convey the comforting message that despite all the awful things which are happening in the world, the new heaven and the new earth will arise - the new Jerusalem.
Christ is victorious!
Conquer with Him through faith in Him!

The decision to publish this book was reached after I realised that my aim was being restricted by simply exhibiting the original paintings. Here, the twenty-four paintings have been reproduced in an artistically sound manner. I am indebted to Pieter Kwant who has encouraged me and is responsible for the publication of this English edition, making this collection accessible to a wider international market. The requests of many people who have seen my work also contributed to this decision. A book which may be looked at, read, and recited, has come into being.

A few words of gratitude:-
In the first place I owe many thanks to my husband who has always supported me and has given me every encouragement in realising this book. I am also very grateful to Piet Krolis who has given my text such a fascinating literary form. My thanks also go to the photographer Dolf Hoving who has put so much effort into making the slides for the lithos. For the translation and correction work, I would like to thank Anne Marie Smith-Buddingh, Jill Bromiley, Gert Riemens, and Rijk van de Kuit. Furthermore I thank Wim van der Geer and Ton Bolland for their very valuable advice, and indeed all those who have contributed in their own way to APOCALYPSE. Thanks also to Invicta Press for their cooperation and excellent graphics.

THE REVELATION
OF JOHN,
the last book of the Bible,
is a complex book
full of mystery and mysticism.

But to reveal
is to unveil.
And God's Plan
of the things to come
was unveiled to John,
the prophet and apostle,
in visions,
on the island of Patmos,
his place of exile

The veil was lifted
and he was able to see.
He saw awesome things:
judgement and rejection,
blood and fire,
and wars;
the empire of Satan,
perishing.

And the empire of Satan _is_ perishing.
Victory belongs
to the Lamb who was slain.

There are images of the indescribable,
of the Wonderful,
of the Eternal,
of the Throne
and the angels around it;
of the redeemed
in white robes;
of tears wiped away;
of elders numbering twenty-four...

...a number that also counts
these paintings.
They closely trace the script
of that strange book
REVELATION:
The Unrivalled Epic.

T he veil is removed
for the great future
....
first for the Son
Jesus Christ,
God and Man,
Mediator
between God and mankind.
The Son reveals it
to his angel,
and the angel shows John
what is
and what will be.

Write John!
Write what you see
and what you hear!

BLESSED ARE THOSE
WHO HEAR THE WORD
AND TAKE IT TO HEART

AND BLESSED ARE THOSE
WHO READ IT.

Revelation 1: 1-3

On the day of the Lord
John went into a trance
in the Spirit.
And looking behind him
he sees...
seven golden lampstands,
and among them a figure
like a son of MAN,
dressed in a robe
down to his feet;
around his chest
a golden sash;
hair like wool,
as white as snow;
eyes like blazing fire;
a sharp, double-edged sword
coming out of his mouth.
His feet
are like burnished bronze,
his voice
the sound of rushing waters.
He holds seven stars
in his right hand.
His face
is the splendour
of the sun.

SON OF MAN,
SON OF GOD!
Is that JESUS?
John recognises Him
and falls down
as though dead.

Then Jesus,
who was dead,
but lives forever
stretches out his right hand
to comfort him
and encourage him.

Christ tells John
that the seven lampstands,
are the seven churches,
united with their Lord,
who is surely in their midst.
And the seven stars
are the leaders
of those seven churches.
Angels, they are called.
Seven, the symbol of fullness.

Revelation 1: 10-20

I ncredible things take place.
A DOOR IN HEAVEN
IS OPENED!
John sees...
we see...
a Mighty Throne
with SOMEONE seated there,
sparkling like a diamond,
and like carnelian,
a stone as red
as the blood of life.
Seven colours encircle the throne:
a rainbow,
the symbol of God's covenant;
and shimmering in front,
a sea of glass,
as clear as crystal.

But look and listen,
the Throne is alive:
lightning and thunder;
seven lamps ablaze,
symbols of the Spirit.

We see even more...
things marvellous and unthinkable:
four creatures with wings:
a lion,
an eagle,
a creature with the face of a man,
and an ox.
They are full of eyes;
nothing escapes them.
They bring their Creator
the honour due to Him
"HOLY, HOLY, HOLY,
IS THE LORD GOD,
THE ALMIGHTY,
WHO WAS,
AND IS,
AND IS TO COME."
The twenty-four elders,
in white robes,
and crowns of gold,
seated around the Throne,
sound this praise
on behalf of the churches
of the past, the present, and the future,
and worship Him.

Revelation 4: 1-11

In the hand of the One
who is enthroned in heaven
we see a scroll,
so awesome in content,
that writing appears
on both sides.
It is God's Plan for the world,
concerning what was, what is,
and what is to come.
But that scroll
is securely sealed
seven times.
Only the Eternal
knows its contents.

An angel appears,
a mighty angel.
He shouts this question
into eternity:
"WHO IS WORTHY
TO BREAK THE SEALS
AND OPEN
THE SCROLL?"

Silence descends
around the angel.
No answer comes
from anywhere;
not from earth,
not from heaven.
The silence
overwhelms John.
He weeps and weeps...
....
until one of the elders
tells him of One
who is worthy
to open the scroll
seal by seal:
the Lion of the tribe of Judah,
the Root of David.
But that Lion...
is a Lamb
who was slain,
red with blood:
Jesus Christ,
Lion and Lamb,
slain but standing,
killed
but alive
for ever.
Two in One,
worthy to accept
the scroll
from the right hand
of the Eternal on the throne.
The scroll can be opened
SEAL BY SEAL!

Revelation 5: 1-7

T he FIRST seal
is opened
by the Lamb.

From the deep,
the voice of one of the creatures
thunders
through space,
"C O M E...!"
And ...
a white horse appears.
Its rider draws a bow
and his arrows strike home.
He wears
the crown of victory.

The SECOND SEAL
is opened.
The second creature calls,
"C o m e...!"
And ...
a scarlet horse appears,
scarlet for the blood,
that is to flow.
Its rider has a sword
to take away peace,
so that war will remain.

The THIRD SEAL
is opened.
The third creature calls:
"C o m e...!"
And ...
a pitch-black horse appears,
black for death and famine.
The rider holds
a pair of scales in his hand.
A voice declares,
"A quart of wheat
for a denarius,
three quarts of barley
also for a denarius."
For times will be scarce.

The FOURTH SEAL
is opened.
The fourth creature calls,
"C o m e...!"
And ...
an ugly horse appears,
pale is its colour.
Its rider is Death,
and Hades follows in its wake.
Its task is to kill
one-quarter of the earth.

The FIFTH SEAL opens up
a view of the altar
in heaven.
And ...
beneath it are the souls
of those slain
because of the Word of God.
Their complaint reaches the Holy
One:
"How long have we yet to wait
for the eternal redemption?"
They receive robes,
white and pure,
but they still have to rest
for a short while
until their number is complete.

The SIXTH SEAL
is opened:
The Great Day of God begins
with the end of the world.
The earth trembles as never before.
Stars fall down
like figs from a tree.
The sun has turned dark
like sackcloth made of hair,
and the moon turns blood-red.
As a scroll
the sky recedes...
Make Way!
for A NEW HEAVEN
and A NEW EARTH!

The seventh seal
is not yet opened,
not yet...

Revelation 6: 1-17

F our angels occupy
the ends of the earth,
from where they must
hold back the winds,
so that no storms
will lash the sea and earth,
and the plants shall remain.

And at the rising of the sun
a fifth angel appears.
He has the seal
from God himself,
to mark the heads
of God's servants,
and he calls to the others
to keep holding back
the winds
as long as the number
of Israel's chosen
is not yet complete.
Then John is told
the number of Israel's sealed:
one hundred and forty-four thousand.
All the tribes,
from Judah to Benjamin -
each has twelve thousand
chosen ones.

Twelve times twelve thousand:
a FULL and HOLY number.

Revelation 7: 1-8

T he heavens are full of people
   who have come
   from all directions:
from north and south,
from east and west,
from all peoples and nations,
from across seas and oceans;
white and brown,
yellow and black,
men, women and children,
innumerable people in white robes,
a multitude no-one can count,
like the stars in the sky.

...they stand around the Throne
and the Lamb,
worshipping and waving
palm branches;
a very large choir.
With one voice they praise God
and the Lamb.

The angels, the elders
and the four living creatures,
standing between the Throne
and the multitude,
bow down and worship
before the Throne and the Lamb,
joining their voices
with the large choir of the multitude
and singing the chorus
"Amen! Praise and glory,
wisdom, thanks and honour,
and power and strength
be to our God
for ever and ever!
Amen."

The multitude,
that no-one can count,
worships God
day and night.
They will no longer hunger,
and no longer thirst,
the sun will not beat upon them,
nor the heat of the day,
for the Lamb
at the centre of the Throne
will be their shepherd.

AND GOD WILL WIPE AWAY
EVERY TEAR FROM THEIR EYES.

Revelation 7: 9-17

The Holy One opens
the seventh
and last seal
of the scroll.

An angel appears
at the golden altar of incense.

From the censer
he has poured incense
on the altar;
the fragrant smoke
of the prayers of the saints
goes up from his hand
to the Holy One.

Then the same angel
fills the censer
with fire from the altar
and hurls it on the earth,
so that the earth trembles
and the sky is full
of flashes of lightning
and peals of thunder.

And ...
seven angels with trumpets
take up their places.

The FIRST
SOUNDS THE TRUMPET
and the earth is covered with hail
and fire mixed with blood,
so that one third of the earth
is burned up.

The SECOND
SOUNDS THE TRUMPET
and something like a mountain
falls into the sea, all ablaze,
so that one third
of the sea is turned into blood
and no life
is found there anymore.

The THIRD
SOUNDS THE TRUMPET
a star falls burning
from the sky,
- Wormwood (bitter) is its name -
so that one third of the
springs of water and rivers
are poisoned.

The FOURTH
SOUNDS THE TRUMPET,
and one third of the
sun, moon and stars
are turned dark,
so that the people
can no longer work.

Then an EAGLE appears
flying in mid-air.
From its mouth sounds
threefold woe,
for yet more woes
will be poured out
over the earth.

The FIFTH
SOUNDS THE TRUMPET
and a dark star falls from the sky.
A dark power
opens the shaft of the Abyss.
Thick grey smoke
rises from the chasm,
which is full of locusts,
so that the sun is darkened.

This kind of locust has a face
like a human face,
long hair like a woman's,
and teeth like a lion's;
There is a golden crown on its head,
and it is harnessed in iron,
for it is invulnerable.
It flies with large wings.
Its tail, like that of a scorpion,
has a deadly sting.

The SIXTH
SOUNDS THE TRUMPET.
He must release
the angels of Satan
at the Euphrates;
they are four in number.
A war breaks out;
such has never been before.
Three horses and three riders
are here as their symbols.

The breastplates of the riders
are red like fire
that burns everything,
blue like smoke
that suffocates everything,
and yellow like sulphur
that poisons everything.

And fire, smoke and sulphur
come out of the mouths
of the horses
with heads like lions.
And in their tails,
*like heads of snakes,
is the VENOM.*

The seventh angel
is still far off.
He is yet to come.

Revelation 8: 1-13
9: 1-20

A mighty angel descends from heaven
robed in a cloud,
with a rainbow
around his head.
His face is radiant
like the sun,
and his legs
are like pillars of fire.
Earth and sea
are subjected to him,
for one foot rests on the earth,
the other on the sea.

His voice is the voice
of a roaring lion.
And the sound
of heavy, black thunder
is heard.

But ...
the mighty angel
lifts his right hand
and declares
that the Great Day
 of the Lord
is coming!

 John hears a voice.
 "Go and take the book,
that is lying open
in the hand of
the mighty angel.
Take it
and eat it.
It will be pink
 and as sweet as honey
in your mouth,
but in your stomach
it will be yellow
 and bitter like bile.

John eats the book
and he is commanded
to prophesy again.

Revelation 10: 1-11

J ohn is given a reed
like a measuring rod,
with which he is to measure
the temple and altar,
and those who worship there.

And God sends
his two witnesses
clothed in black sackcloth,
for they must prophesy
for twelve hundred and sixty days.

They both symbolise
olive trees and lampstands;
the oil from the trees
incessantly feeds the lampstands,
so that the gospel
is passed on
through the centuries,
humiliating the proud,
exalting the humble,
discovering and enlightening,
preaching judgement
and mercy
until...

...until the witnesses
have completed their testimony
and the BEAST appears.
From the Abyss it rises.
It kills the two witnesses.
Their bodies remain
lying in the street
as a symbol for everyone,
for they are glad
that the message,
which made them
discover themselves,
may no longer be heard.
They even send
presents to each other:

Congratulations, God is dead!

But when one day has passed,
and one more day,
and yet another day,
and half a day...
Look...
GOD'S SPIRIT enters
the bodies of the witnesses.
They rise
and ascend to heaven
in a cloud.

Then there is
a severe earthquake.
At long last, give God the glory.
those who are still living on earth

Revelation 11: 1-14

The SEVENTH ANGEL
may at last sound the trumpet.
We see
GOD'S ETERNAL KINGDOM
worshipped in an antiphony
by angels,
the twenty-four elders
bowed down before the Throne,
and a countless throng behind them.

Radiant red is the countenance
of the Eternal,
who has risen
from his throne,
for his wrath has now come
because of the wickedness of the nations.
The time of judgement
has come.

But ...
the Temple of God opens.
And the Ark of his covenant
becomes visible to everyone.

And there are flashes of lightning
and peals of thunder.

Revelation 11: 15-19

A great SIGN
can be seen:
a woman,
clothed with the sun,
the moon under her feet,
and a crown of twelve stars
on her head.

The woman is pregnant,
and she cries out in pain
as she gives birth to the Christ-child.

But...what is this
rising from the Abyss?
A demonic beast,
a dragon, like a snake,
as red as blood,
with seven heads, on each a crown,
and ten horns.
Its tail sweeps one third
of the stars to the earth.

The demonic dragon is ready
to devour
the new-born Child,
but the Child
is snatched up to God.

The fury of Satan
is now directed at the woman,
but God allows her
to escape to the desert.

Even in heaven
the dragon still pursues the Child.
But then war breaks out there:
Michael, God's first angel,
and his angels
wage war and conquer.
The dragon and all his devils
are hurled down...
to the earth...
to the people!

Heaven has been closed off
for ever
to Satan and his devils.
Even greater is the fury
of the snake,
who will take revenge
as long as he may and can.

The woman,
the symbol of the Church,
is again Satan's target
and is pursued till the end.
And she would have been devoured
if God had not given her
two wings with which to flee.

In a final attempt
the snake spews
a torrent of water
to overtake the woman.
But the earth opens its mouth;
the torrent is swallowed up in it,
so that the woman escapes!

Revelation 12: 1-18

30

From the depths of the sea
a beast is born, horrible to behold ,
with seven heads,
and ten crowned horns,
and on its heads
are blasphemous names.
The beast, resembling a leopard,
has feet like those of a bear,
and a mouth like that of a lion.
Its power
comes from the red demonic dragon,
who was thrown down,
for the beast of the sea is its slave.
Common to both
are the seven heads.
Seven heads:
seven successive world powers.

One head is fatally wounded,
but miraculously it is healed!
And anyone
whose name has not been written
in the book of the Lamb who was slain,
worships the beast
and the image of the beast,
which the people have erected.

The earth too brings forth a beast,
apparently as sweet as a lamb;
with its two horns
remarkably like the Lamb.
But it must not open its mouth,
for it speaks the language
of the dragon.

It is the slave
of the beast
that came out of the sea,
and it deceives the people
into worshipping the beast of the sea
and its image,
which has been given "life"
by the beast
which came out of the earth.

As a reward these people receive
a mark on their right hand
or forehead,
a sign of association
with the beast.
THE MARK OF THE BEAST,
is a number:
six hundred and sixty six,
because it is not quite
what it wants to be...
GOD'S NUMBER:
seven hundred and seventy seven,
and that very similarity
makes it so dangerous.

But look, three angels are
flying there;
one angel
with the eternal gospel,
a second
who predicts the fall of Babylon,
and a third
who warns everyone
about worshipping the beast
and its image.

But ...
Blessed are the dead
who die in the Lord
from now on.
"Yes," says the Spirit
"they will rest from their labour,
for their deeds will follow them."

Revelation   13: 1-18
              14: 6-13

A nd look, look...
...on Zion's holy mountain
there is the Lamb!
And around the throne
there on that mountain,
there in heaven
are the angels, the four creatures,
and THE ONE HUNDRED AND
FORTY FOUR THOUSAND
who have been sealed.

And listen, listen...
they are singing
a NEW SONG,
never heard before;
great and majestic
like the sound
of rushing waters,
accompanied
by many harps.

*These are the ones
who follow the Lamb
wherever He goes.
They were purchased
from among men as the firstfruits
to God and the Lamb.*

Revelation 14: 1-5

Who is seated
on the white cloud?
It is the Son of God,
the Son of Man.
There is a crown of gold
on his head
and a sickle in his hand.

An angel comes out of the temple,
and calls to Him there on the cloud:
"Use your sickle
and reap the corn,
for the harvest is ripe."
And the earth is harvested.

A second angel comes out of
the temple,
a sickle in his hand.

A third angel,
who is in charge
of the fire on the altar,
commands the angel with the sickle,
"Gather the clusters of grapes."

And the harvest
from the vineyard of the earth
is thrown
into the great winepress
of God's wrath,
which is outside the city.
And a river of wine like blood
reaches as high as the horse's bridle:
sixteen hundred stadia,
one hundred and eighty miles.

Revelation 14: 14-20

A wondrous
heavenly sign
is seen
and heard:
the choir of victors
- those who did not kneel
to the beast, nor to its image -
beside the temple
at the sea of glass mixed with fire,
playing their harps
and singing the jubilant song of Moses.

As these sounds fade into the distance,
we see the temple being opened.
Seven angels appear there;
their clothes are shining,
their sashes made of gold.

One of the four creatures
gives the seven angels
seven golden bowls
full of God's wrath.
Smoke fills the temple.

The FIRST ANGEL
empties his golden bowl
onto the land,
and ugly sores break out
on people and animals.

The SECOND ANGEL
empties his golden bowl
on the sea,
which becomes like blood
so that no life
is found there any longer.

The THIRD ANGEL
empties his golden bowl
on the rivers and the springs;
the water there
becomes deadly blood.

The FOURTH ANGEL
empties his golden bowl
on the sun,
which causes
scorching and searing
as never before.

The FIFTH ANGEL
pours out his golden bowl
on the throne
of the awful satanic beast,
so that his domain
is darkened
but not yet destroyed.

The SIXTH ANGEL
pours out his golden bowl
on the Euphrates,
so that its bed dries up
and the way is prepared
for the kings and their armies,
who come
from where the sun rises
to destroy
the people of God.

But ...
The satanic dragon,
the beast from the sea
and the beast that came
from the earth,
these three each spew out creatures:
three unclean frogs
come out of their mouths.
These are the demonic spirits
who give rise
to the great battle of nations,
the war on the Great Day
of the Almighty.

And the SEVENTH pours out
his bowl into the air.
A loud voice proclaims:
"It is done!"
And with these words
peals of thunder resound;
we see flashes of lightning
and huge hailstones;
the earth trembles and groans
until the end.

Revelation 15: 1- 8
16: 1-21

One of the angels,
who had poured out
a golden bowl of wrath,
leads John in the Spirit
into the desert.

Seated on a red scarlet beast
covered with blasphemy,
and resembling the beast,
that came from the sea,
is a woman, flaunting herself,
a prostitute,
dressed in purple and scarlet,
decorated with gold and pearls,
and with diamonds.
The mark on her forehead shows
that she has much to hide.

The great prostitute is out
to seduce the world
for her master, Satan,
and to lead them away from God
and from the Lamb.
Yes, she and the red beast
intend to kill the Lamb
and his Church.
She is drunk from the blood
of God's witnesses;
her cup runs over.

The great prostitute,
Babylon the great -
the symbol of Satan's headquarters,
is seated on the beast
with the seven heads.
Seven heads: seven hills,
seven kings,
the seven world-powers,
who succeed each other.
They are also the seven waves
of the large sea of nations
which has been seduced by the prostitute.

The scarlet beast grows another head,
coming forth from one of the seven:
the total Antichrist,
victorious....
until the final battle,
for this will be won
by the Lamb.

Then the angel,
who illuminates the earth,
calls from heaven,
"Fallen, fallen
is the great city of
BABYLON!"

And look...
Babylon the Great, the prostitute,
burns, and disappears forever.
Smoke and a bit of ash
are all that remains,
to the great dismay
of those who gained
their wealth from her:
kings,
ships'crews ,
and merchants.

A mighty angel
throws a millstone into the sea
with great violence,
for this is how Babylon
will disappear,
and no-one will find her again.

Revelation 17: 1-18
18: 1-24

40

But listen, and look...
there is a great multitude
singing
like the roar
of rushing waters:

"Hallelujah,
for the Lord God Almighty reigns
for ever and ever.
Let us rejoice and be glad,
for the wedding of the Lamb
is fast approaching.
It is the wedding of the Lamb,
of Christ ,
and of his bride
which is the Church,
manifest in fine linen,
clean and white"

Beside her is the wedding feast:
BLESSED ARE THOSE WHO ARE INVITED
TO THE WEDDING FEAST
OF THE LAMB!

John is so overwhelmed
by this vision
that he kneels to worship the angel,
who has shown him all this.
But angels
are no more than messengers
from and for the Lord -
they are servants too.

Revelation 19: 6-10   TO GOD ALONE BE THE GLORY!

Heaven is opened
once more.
A white horse appears.
Its Knight is Christ
and he is called
Faithful and True.
His eyes are like blazing fire.
His head is covered
with many crowns.
He wields an iron rod,
and out of his mouth
comes a double-edged sword.
He treads the winepress.
His robe has been dipped in blood,
and these words are written
on his thigh:
"King of kings,
Lord of lords".

He and his procession
dressed in white
and on white horses,
wage war
against the beasts from the sea
and from the earth
and their scarlet armies.

But they are thrown down,
by the Knight on his white horse,
into the eternal fire.

*There is another angel
standing there in the sun;
he calls the birds
flying in mid-air
to eat the flesh
of those who have been rejected.*

*And all the birds
ate their fill.*

Revelation   19:11-21

An angel descends from heaven
with the key to the Abyss
and a great chain
in his hand.

He seizes the red dragon
and throws him into the Abyss,
where he is kept prisoner
for A THOUSAND YEARS.

And look...
there are thrones
where the jury is seated,
for the authority to judge
has been given to them.

And look...
there are the souls
of those who were beheaded
because they testified of their Lord,
but they were woken up,
and reigned with Christ
as priests and kings
for those one thousand years.

But when the thousand years
are over,
Satan breaks loose,
and gathers all the nations
from the corners of the earth.
They lay siege to the camp,
the beloved city
where God's people
are gathered.

But when all seems lost,
the Almighty intervenes again.
He throws the dragon,
the beast and the false prophet
into the lake of fire
where they will burn
forever.

Revelation 20: 1-10

When the first heaven
has passed away,
and the first earth too
and everything has disappeared,
the Throne remains,
great and white;
there God's Majesty is enthroned.

And standing there
before that majestic throne
are the DEAD,
the great, but also the small.
They have come from everywhere;
the sea gives them up,
and Hades too.

Books are opened,
and then another:
THE LAMB'S BOOK OF LIFE.
Then all is revealed -
all that everyone has done
or has not done in their lives,
or should have done.

And each one
is judged accordingly.

Revelation 20: 11-15

An angel leads John
in the Spirit
to a high mountain top,
where he sees,
that the first heaven
and the first earth
have passed away.
But he sees more...
He sees much more;
John sees
the NEW JERUSALEM,
the holy city,
coming down from heaven,
dressed like a bride,
adorned like a bride,
a city with the face of a bride,
veiled with God's glory,
radiating like a diamond.

The angel measures the city
with a measuring rod of gold.
It is square;
the length, the width and the height
are each one hundred and forty-four
stadia.
In each of the four walls
there are three gates,
and each of the gates is named
after one of the twelve tribes
of Israel.
Pearly are the gates
and they are never closed.
Twelve angels keep watch there.

The city's foundations
are decorated with precious stones:
jasper, sapphire,
chalcedony and emerald,
sardonyx and carnelian,
topaz, beryl,
chrysolite and chrysoprase,
jacinth and amethyst.
The twelve foundations each
bear the name of an apostle.
The streets of the city
are of pure gold
and transparent like glass.

There is no temple
in this Jerusalem,
for God
and the Lamb
are its Temple.
Sunlight and moonlight
are no longer seen
through the radiance
of God's glory,
and the Lamb is its lamp.

Out of the throne
flows a spring of living water,
as clear as crystal.
It flows on as a river.
Along its banks are trees of life.
They blossom
twelve months of the year.
That is ETERNAL LIFE!

Eternally
the saints live there.
Eternally
they rule with Him.
They give Him glory eternally!

And He will wipe every tear
from their eyes,
and there will be no more death
or mourning, or crying
or pain,
for the former of things
have passed away.
And He who is seated on the throne
says: "Behold! I make all things new".

Revelation 21:1- 5, 9-27
            22:1- 5

I AM
the Alpha and the Omega,
the First and the Last,
the Beginning and the End,
the Almighty and the Eternal.

He who is
He who was
and He who is to come.

Revelation 1: 8
                 22:13

With blessing He left -
With blessing He will come!

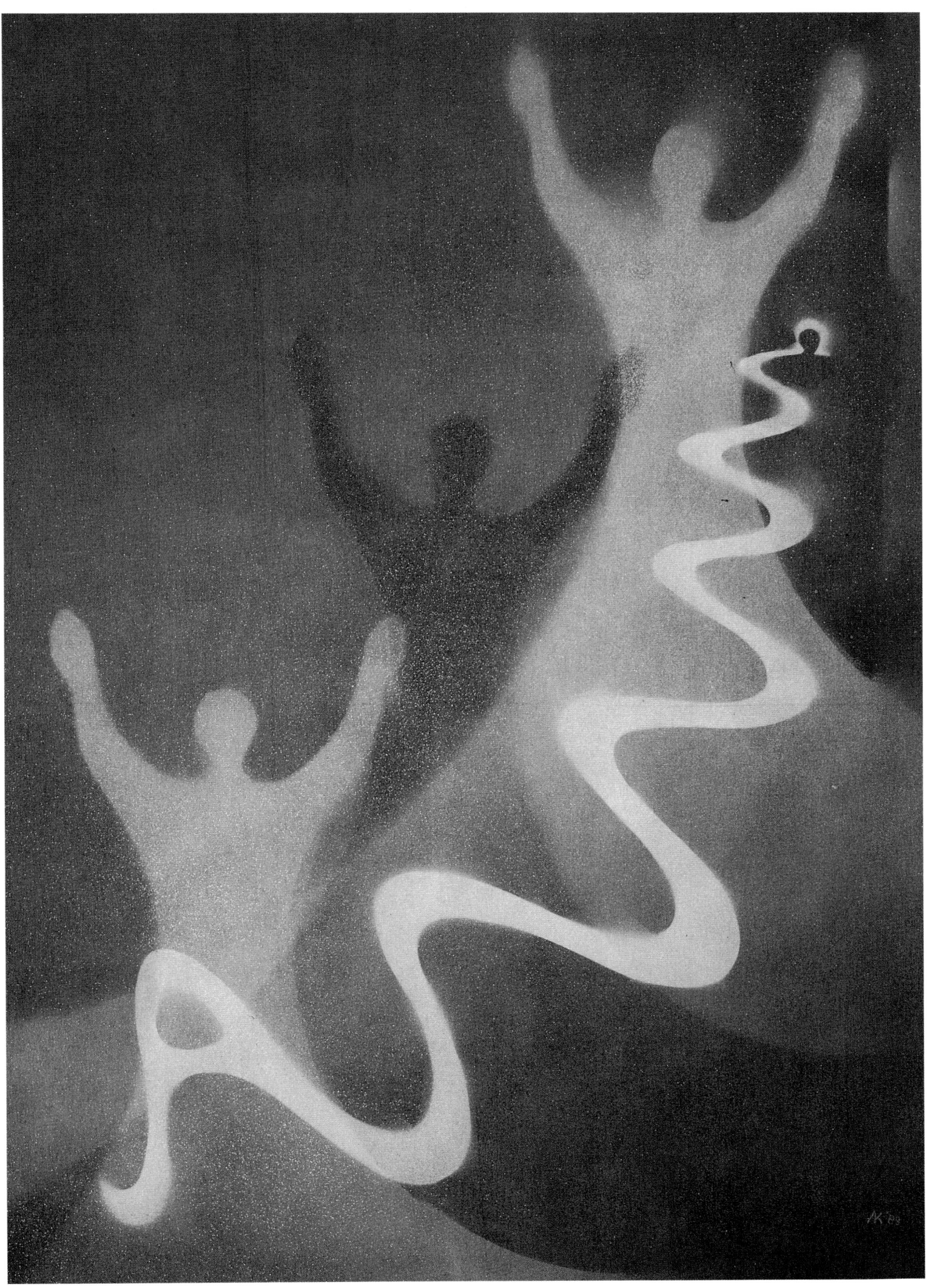

Blue darkness,
a star;
all fear has disappeared,
and peace has taken its place.
In the heavens
shines the Bright Morning Star:
JESUS.

Even though we do not always
see that star,
because there are clouds,
or the earth obscures her,
it is there -
Christ is there,
the Lord is there,
always,
faithful,
throughout the ages
until THE GREAT DAY.
His radiance
is already beginning to shine through.

HE
WHO TESTIFIES TO THESE THINGS
SAYS,
 "YES, I AM COMING SOON."

AMEN. COME, LORD JESUS!

The grace of the Lord Jesus Christ
be with you all.

Revelation 22: 16c, 20 and 21

Anneke Kaai, nee van Wijngaarden, was born in Naarden on 5th February, 1951. She received her training at the "Gooise Academie voor Beeldende Kunsten", and continued her studies at the "Gerrit Rietveld Academie" in Amsterdam.
Inspired by the Bible and her faith, Anneke's work can be described as semi-abstract, embracing much Christian symbolism. She has painted a sequence on The Creation (15), The Ten Commandments (12), and Revelation (24 - visionally realistic). Exhibitions of her paintings are frequently held and her work has been reviewed on television several times.
The paintings are now property of bv Bouwbureau Brandwijk, Sliedrecht, The Netherlands.

Also published by Anneke Kaai: De Schepping in Beeld.

Original title: Openbaring in Beeld.

© Copyright 1992 - Anneke Kaai
Translation © Copyright 1992 - Anne Marie Smith-Buddingh / Jill Bromily
This English edition published by arrangement with the author Utrechtsestraatweg 64, 3911 TW Rhenen,
The Netherlands, Tel.:08376-12354 and the Printer Drukkerij Invicta, Addenshoeve 9, 3911 TG Rhenen,
The Netherlands.

British Library Cataloguing in Publication Data -

Kaai, Anneke
Apocalypse: Meditations of the Revelation of John in Word and Picture
I. Title
228
ISBN 0-85364-550-7

Typeset and printed in The Netherlands for The Paternoster Press, PO Box 300, Carlisle, Cumbria, CA3 0QZ,
by Drukkerij Invicta, Addenshoeve 9, 3911 TG Rhenen.